TOUCHDOWN
FINANCE

TOUCHDOWN
FINANCE

PERSONAL FINANCE TIPS FROM THE PROS

DR. JOHN KARAFFA

CPA/PFS, CFP®

ISBN 978-1-54394-931-5 (print)

ISBN 978-1-54394-932-2 (ebook)

For information on quantity discounts and requests for permission of use, please e-mail TaxPro@ProSportCPA.com.

This book is dedicated to all the professional athletes who taught me what they have learned about making good financial decisions. Hopefully their lessons of what to do and what not to do will help others make better choices.

CONTENTS

Introduction

PREGAME

If you're a sports fan, you've read or heard about professional athletes and their money. In the United States, professional sports is a multi-billion dollar industry, with the NFL alone hauling in $13 billion in reported 2016 revenue. Sports is big business, and some professional athletes are making millions of dollars. Athletes, like the rest of the working world, are faced with big financial decisions. Some make good choices, and some make poor choices.

I've had an inside view of athletes and their finances for several decades. I was a professional basketball player for twelve seasons in Germany and New Zealand, after graduating from Butler University in Indiana. I am also a Certified Public Accountant and Certified Financial Planner®, and now lead my own firm, ProSport CPA, which has served more than one thousand sports professionals. I've seen the challenges from both sides of the game, and I think we can all learn something from these pros.

Yes, many pro athletes have more zeros at the end of their paychecks than you or I do, but that just means their decisions create amplified results. Success or failure happens in a shorter span of time.

That shorter timeframe, coupled with the immense notoriety that professional athletes garner, allows us to see patterns more clearly, which may help us see weaknesses in our own financial decisions. It is much easier on the pocketbook to learn from others' mistakes!

My doctoral dissertation is titled *Retired National Football League Players' Perceptions of Financial Decisions Made: A Phenomenological Study*. If that doesn't sound like gripping reading, have no fear. The academic title hides the essence: how former pros felt about their spending habits, their knowledge of personal finance, and their insight into financial decisions.

I noticed some significant patterns when working on my dissertation. I chose to study the financial decisions of former NFL players. What would they say were their best decisions? How did they manage their money when playing and after their sports careers ended? What would they do differently? What advice would they offer to others?

I see so much value in what I learned from interviewing those twenty-five NFL pros. I am still learning through my interaction with professional athletes my firm serves. I've gleaned some significant patterns and created some financial rules that I pass on to clients. I now want to pass them on to you. Since personal finance books aren't always the most exciting to read, I hope the sports stories and lessons I've learned from these pros will peak your interest.

When I set up my accounting firm, I wanted a business that people could trust, that would help athletes with more than just taxes. My objective remains to guide our clients on the road to financial success and peace of mind so they make better financial decisions.

I want you to experience that same success. I want you to know where your money is going, to be wise financially, and to avoid the pitfalls that some of these pros have made. That's what this book is about—learning from each other on and off the field.

This book is organized into seven chapters. Each represents a theme that former pros shared. These chapters, or rules, will serve as the guidelines for you to realize financial success. Here's a sneak peek at the game plan:

Rule 1: Take It Slow

When it comes to finances, you'll be playing smarter if you don't rush into big decisions. Learn all you can while you save your money and limit your spending to things you actually need. Concentrate on lowering your debt and living within your means.

Rule 2: Budget and Save

Putting these two principles into practice can change your whole financial picture. When you make a budget and stick to it, you keep yourself from making financial choices that might hurt you. When you save, you have money. It's not being spent and not being lost on a risky investment. You will never lose if you budget and save.

Rule 3: Educate Yourself

The world of personal finance can be tricky. You're off to a good start by reading this book because you're taking time to learn about principles that will help you for a lifetime. When you understand your net worth, you can tackle your weak spots and focus on improving areas of finance that seem confusing to you.

Rule 4: Consult Trustworthy Professionals

Recruit a strong team of people you trust to help you succeed and meet your goals. Very few people will be able to make all the financial choices they face without strong guidance. You should take the lead, but let qualified accountants, financial planners, and investment advisors help you.

Rule 5: Protect Your Assets

Consider this to be the "Just Say No" chapter. You will save yourself a lot of financial headaches and heartaches if you make life-changing decisions, like marriage and parenting, only when you're ready for these commitments. You also need to protect the money you have for long-term use and not give it or loan it without proper consideration.

Rule 6: Plan Your Future

Your money needs to last as long as you do! Recognize that life comes in stages. Preparing when you're young and being realistic about your senior years means that you can live comfortably in retirement. No one wants financial stress to follow them through life. You can avoid it if you plan accordingly for your needs.

Rule 7: Stick To Safe Investments

I put the chapter on investing at the end of the book, because I believe that so many other financial principles need to come first. When you're ready, making safe investments can be very rewarding and something that secures your winning financial future.

I hope you will implement some or all of these rules in your life so you can win with your personal finances. Good luck to each of you!

RULE 1

TAKE IT SLOW

BE CONSERVATIVE AND PROTECT YOUR MONEY WHILE DEVELOPING FINANCIAL GOALS

Anyone who makes a lot of money very quickly without strong financial instincts or education will face challenges. This is certainly true for young athletes who are suddenly making big league money. In my years serving football players early in their NFL careers, I've noticed two common approaches to their paychecks—spend it or save it.

Some were so excited to have money that they slipped into the "keeping up with the Joneses" mindset—big houses, tricked-out cars, gold jewelry, family members and friends on the payroll. These athletes were aggressive with spending and, sometimes, investing.

Others were overwhelmed with the money and took a cautious approach. One former pro told me he was afraid to spend his rookie salary. The cautious spenders sounded almost apologetic, as if they expected me to support aggressive investments right away.

This is a great guiding principle and Rule 1 for us all. If you don't know what to do with money, saving it is always safe. If you're saving it, you're not spending it. If you're not spending it, you're not wasting it.

Taking it slowly is a building block of good personal financial decisions. When you get money, no matter how little or how much, spend carefully. Don't make big decisions right away. Wait until you've done your research and are confident. Save, save, save. You can't go wrong with saving.

This chapter might seem like common sense. *Take it slow. Don't make big purchases or try to hit an investment home run right away.* But this is what I've experienced and observed with people who suddenly have money: it doesn't feel right *not* to spend it. They often feel an urgency to spend or invest. The same is true for college graduates or anyone else in the workforce.

Rather than dealing with the stress of overspending or managing unwieldly investments, why not keep it simple? Finish your education, build a career, develop relationships, and grow your network. If you give into the burning desire to spend your money, you might miss those important foundational pieces that pay significant dividends throughout your life.

The idea of moving slowly doesn't apply only to those who are receiving their first paychecks. It's relevant anytime you receive more money than you have in the past. When you get a new job, raise, or promotion, or your business starts to thrive, or you're trying to change poor spending habits, it's time to learn some new skills. Just as in sports, it takes time for players to learn new plays and then practice and perfect them for the game. Take it slow and build a strong foundation for your financial future.

Many professional athletes have some learning to do about slowing down and protecting their money. One of the most dramatic examples that played out in the public eye revolved around a bad investment in an Alabama entertainment and gambling development. Financial advisor Jeff Rubin persuaded dozens of NFL players, including all-pro running back Fred Taylor and tight end Vernon Davis, to invest in Country Crossing, a casino that was basing its proposed revenue on electronic bingo machines. But two weeks after opening in January 2010, the machines were ruled illegal in the state and were confiscated by Alabama law enforcement. When the venue went bankrupt, NFL players lost a combined $43 million in investments.

The players could have protected themselves by not making a rush decision to invest in the casino. Though Rubin presented it as an opportunity to get very rich, the players could have taken the time to notice warning signs. The NFL Commissioner Roger Goodell and Alabama Governor Bob Riley were both strongly opposed to gambling. There was also a statement in a document given to potential investors that the electronic gambling machines might be considered illegal. This disastrous investment is, to date, the largest financial loss of NFL players tied to one financial advisor. It is better to learn from others' mistakes.

AVOID THE BLITZ OF EXCESSIVE SPENDING: NEEDS VS. WANTS

Before we get to financial concepts like budgeting, saving, and goal setting, I want to emphasize two skills that are essential for you to understand and master. Think of me as a coach for a minute, emphasizing some basic foundational concepts of the game.

You need to clearly understand and respect the fundamental difference between a *need* and a *want*.

What are needs?
- A place to live
- Appropriate clothes
- Food on the table
- Transportation
- Basic necessities for living safely and securely

What are wants masquerading as needs?
- A large, new home
- A luxury vehicle
- First-class plane tickets
- Expensive clothing and shoes
- Jewelry

You get the idea.

I've seen a lot of athletes and non-athletes convince themselves that they must spend a lot of money to fit into the world of professional sports. They join the world of name-brand clothes, expensive jewelry, flashy cars, and excessive bills at bars and restaurants. Depending on your career or level of income, you can fall into some of those traps as well.

NBA star Antoine Walker made more than $108 million in his career but filed for bankruptcy just two years after retirement. Involved in gambling and a real estate firm that collapsed, Walker has also publicly said that he got drawn to a very expensive lifestyle that cost him millions at the beginning of his career. Walker consistently lived beyond his means.

In contrast, Alfred Morris of the Dallas Cowboys has made millions during his NFL career but drives a 1991 Mazda, a car he bought in college for two dollars from his pastor. In an interview with ESPN, he explained a sentimental attachment to the car but also said he doesn't see the need for a new car while this one gets him from point A to point B. "You never know when it's going to be over. I'm just doing my best to try to save as much as I can, to set myself up for life after football," Morris said in the interview.

A good question to ask yourself with any purchase is, "if I give it the weekend to think about it, would I be proud of this purchase, or would I question having spent money on it?" Do I *need* it or do I *want* it? Curtailing spontaneous purchases is important. Take it slow and evaluate your *needs*.

STIFF-ARMING DEBT: GOOD DEBT VS. BAD DEBT

It's important to know when it's OK or not OK to borrow money. Larger purchases like cars and houses are usually made with a loan, which means the borrower is now in debt. The biggest reason people borrow money from financial institutions is because they don't have enough lump sum cash for those purchases. Few of us will ever have enough cash on hand to buy a house, or even a car, outright. Loans can help us buy what we need and spread the payments into manageable chunks.

A loan is an obligation, also called a debt, because you must pay it back. When you are lent money at a certain rate of interest, you pay it off over time. The interest paid to the lender is your cost of taking out a loan. The lump sum you owe on the loan is also called debt.

The lender reports to the credit-reporting agencies how you live up to the terms of the loan. This is the basis of your credit score.

The faster you pay back debt, the better your credit score becomes. The better your score, the more likely you are to qualify for loans in the future.

I advise my clients that there are good types of debt and bad types. Some financial advisors argue that all debt is bad, and I respect that viewpoint. However, borrowing money is a necessity for most of us. If done wisely, it will not hurt us financially.

This goes back to needs versus wants. A loan on a car or purchasing a modest house or condo would potentially be good debt, whereas taking out a loan to buy jewelry, an excessive car, or a big house is bad debt.

Good debt

> Auto loan for reasonable car
> School loan to further your education
> Mortgage on a modest home or condo

Bad debt

> Credit card debt (usually with 20 percent interest)
> Luxury car, boat, or jewelry loans
> Mortgages on mansions or custom homes
> Personal lines of credit

Consider these things when taking on debt and avoid the penalties:

- Interest rates. It's worth shopping around with lenders and finding the best rate. The interest rate affects the monthly payment and how long it will take you to pay off the loan.

- Affordable monthly payments. If you have a home loan, you should aim for all your debt payments to be no more than one-third of your take-home pay.

- Credit scores. Loans are tied to your credit scores, and interest rates will vary based on your score. Prove to lenders that you are credit worthy, and you'll receive better rates on your loans.

- Tax breaks. Tax deductions lower the amount of income the government taxes you on, thereby lowering the net amount you pay. Some loans are tax deductible. Home ownership is highly valued in America, so the tax laws allow the deduction of interest paid toward purchasing a home. Other loans like car loans, personal loans, credit cards, and cash loans don't provide that tax benefit.

Here is a chart depicting the various types of loans, their usual rates of interest, and tax deductibility.

Type of debt	Interest rates	Tax deductible
Pay-day loans	20%-600%	No
Credit cards	10%-22%	No
Personal loans	4%-25%	No
Auto loans	4%-8%	No
Home equity line of credit	4%-8%	Yes
Student loans	3%-8%	Yes
Home mortgages	3%-6%	Yes

The discussion of needs and wants and taking on only good debt provides foundation for financial well-being. Master these skills and you will rack up points on the scoreboard. I share with my clients that it is completely OK to "Take It Slow" and live like a college student when starting a career. Others may label you as frugal, but that's a good reputation to have. Those who aren't frugal often are over-extended financially and end up broke. It's like the story of the tortoise and the hare. We all know who won that race!

—— PLAYBOOK ——

RULE 1: TAKE IT SLOW

KEY FUNDAMENTALS:
Don't rush financial decisions
Consider needs vs. wants
Understand good vs. bad debt

TAKE IT FROM A PRO

I was always tight with money. Growing up I would hide my nickels and dimes. I guess I saw my mother like that. She taught me to save my money. I never overspent. I just didn't want all the things that other people wanted. I've always had enough.

The main things that I really wanted, I went and got. I wanted a nice home and a nice car. But if something was going to hurt me, I just didn't go after it. I grew up struggling, we were on welfare for a time, and I didn't ever want to be in that position again.

- Jerry Harkness, National Collegiate Athletic Association (NCAA) basketball national champion at Loyola University Chicago (1963), National Basketball Association (NBA) (1963-1969)

RULE 2

BUDGET AND SAVE

SET GOALS, BEAT THEM, AND WATCH YOUR WEALTH GROW

Budgeting and saving have a reputation as some of the least engrossing topics of personal finance. Financial experts have presented these topics as something you must do, but the reality is you might not be inclined to budget and save. Budgeting and saving need to become habits that follow simple guidelines and rules leading you to do the right thing consistently over time—and win. That's my objective—to coach fundamentals you can use to win the game of wealth.

Budgeting and saving are like free throws, which I used to consider one of the most mundane aspects of basketball. I will never forget playing in the Anderson Wigwam in 1985 for the Noblesville Millers against the Kokomo Wildcats. This game was the regional finals of the infamous Indiana high school basketball tournament. In front of a crowd of around nine thousand spectators, I was fouled going up for a last-second layup. I had the opportunity to either tie the game or help win the game. Unfortunately, I missed the front end of a one-and-one, and we lost that night. From then on, free throws became a big part of my future success as a basketball player. In fact, I helped my Butler University college team lead the nation in free-throw shooting during my freshman and senior years.

Even though worth only one point, free-throw points can be the difference between winning and losing. Free throws are a critical aspect of basketball but often are overlooked. Teams that are better prepared perform better in tight games. They come through in the clutch.

Budgeting and saving might also seem like tedious practices, but don't overlook them. Practicing and becoming extremely proficient at these fundamentals will help you score points every time. **Budgeting and saving are invaluable skills that lead to success, something you can count on to serve you for a lifetime.**

I've seen folks with very little money amass significant wealth by following basic budgeting and saving techniques. They started early, even when their income was small, but they were consistent over time. Their consistency paid off with financial success.

Along with the many ways you can spend your money, you're bombarded with television, magazine, and internet articles about how to invest. Advertisers go into great detail about specific investment vehicles, strategy, risk, and return. While investing is important, the greatest investments won't outpace the fundamentals.

It really won't matter if you get 6 percent, 8 percent, or 10 percent investment returns if you don't create much to invest. Investing alone without a solid base of budgeting and saving won't set you up for the future. It will cause you to become dependent on investment success as opposed to financial success. Taking riskier moves will leave you at the mercy of the financial markets. If you must swing for the fences to try to hit home runs, you will strike out a lot more.

PLAY TO WIN THROUGH BUDGETS

Budgeting is a fundamental skill that is invaluable to your personal finances. Every year I visit coach Tom Shaw at Disney's Wide World of Sports Complex in Orlando, Florida. Coach Shaw is world-renown for teaching athletes speed. He's helped some of the fastest athletes in the world, like former NFL players Deion Sanders and Chris Johnson.

Coach Shaw's focus is simple: improved speed equals improved performance. He teaches athletes to run relaxed, take longer strides, and develop explosive starts. Through intense methodical direction, Coach Shaw has created a successful speed-training system that athletes seek out. Speed is essential to sports, and athletes know that.

Similarly, budgeting is fundamental to personal finance. It's a basic principle. When budgeting gets better, personal finances improve. You might consider it a killjoy or something complicated and confusing. In fact, budgeting is simply the financial technique of tracking, analyzing, and monitoring inflows and outflows of money. It doesn't have to be complicated or scary, and best of all, you get to make all the choices.

Let me try to simplify budgeting for you.

Know where your money is going. The first step is understanding where you spend your money. This will give you a baseline. The best predictor of the future is the past, so look at how you spent your money yesterday, last week, last month, and in the past year. Consider people who are trying to lose weight. One of the best things they can do is write down everything they eat. Seeing it in print makes it feel more real and can even be shocking. Athletes do this so they can track what calories they are consuming. When you write it down,

11

you can't fool yourself. The data is there in black and white. Although basic, whenever you write it down and analyze it, you'll find it easier to look back and judge your decisions.

Tracking spending is a lot like counting calories. You need to know where the good and bad decisions are in order to make changes. You've got to be able to answer these questions: How do I spend my money? Was my money spent on the right things? What should I have done? Some expenses, like your mortgage or rent, are easier to track because you pay the same amount every month. What you spend eating out, buying clothes, or traveling is harder to track. Those numbers can vary greatly, and sometimes you grossly underestimate what has been spent. You could be left wondering where all your money has gone.

I encourage my clients to use a credit card and not pay for things in cash because those transactions are harder to track. When you use a credit card, debit card, check, or a bank transfer, you have an electronic record of your spending. This also makes the Internal Revenue Service (IRS) happy. Tax authorities are not keen on granting tax deductions for cash transactions.

Software programs like Intuit's Quicken or Mint allow you to download all your transactions from your banking website directly into the software. Just seeing where you spend is sometimes a learning experience. You don't need to be particularly computer savvy. These programs are getting easier and easier to use. Find one that works for you. Once the data is in the software, you can categorize the transactions and see where your money has gone.

You can also track your spending manually and log your inflows and outflows as shown below to see where your money goes.

Monthly Inflows/Outflows

Inflows

Employment	Gross Salary	2,000
Employment	Gross Salary (Spouse)	2,000
Invesments	Interest & Dividends	25
Other		
Other		
Other		

Total Inflows — 4,025

Outflows

Taxes	US Federal Tax Withholdings	500
Taxes	US Social Security & Medicare	305
Taxes	State Tax Withholdings	100
Household	Rent	1,200
Household	Mortgage	
Household	Utilities	250
Household	Cell Phone	75
Meals	Groceries	300
Meals	Dining Out	100
Insurance	Health Insurance	300
Insurance	Life Insurance	25
Insurance	Auto Insurance	50
Auto	Car Payment	400
Auto	Gas	100
Auto	Repairs & Maintenance	25
Auto	Tolls, Parking, Etc.	
Education	Tuition	
Education	Student Loans	50
Children	Daycare	
Children	School Costs	
Discretionary	Entertainment	75
Discretionary	Gifts & Hobbies	25
Discretionary	Vacation	
Savings	Company Retirement Plan, 401(k)	100
Savings	Emergency Fund Savings	20
Other		
Other		
Other		

Total Outflows — 4,000

Monthly Surplus/(Deficit) — 25

This is what a budget could look like for a couple who both work and rent an apartment. As you can see, they have $4,025 coming in each month and $4,000 going out. They have a monthly surplus, but it's not much.

You will benefit from completing this worksheet for your own income and expenditures. A blank version of the Monthly Inflows/Outflows template is available for you to download at TouchdownFinance.com. Take the time to complete it using your personal finance information so you can see how you're doing.

Analyze your spending. Once you know how you're spending your money, you can make wise financial changes or decisions. You'll see exactly what's happened in the past and make decisions about the future. I suggest sitting down every month and looking through the different categories. It's best to group your expenditures, putting them into categories that make sense to you and your life. Here are some common groupings to consider: Taxes; Household (rent, mortgage, utilities); Auto (car payment, gas, maintenance, tolls, parking); Meals; Insurance (health, life, car); Education (tuition, student loans); Children (daycare, school); Discretionary (entertainment, gifts, hobbies, vacation); and even Savings (retirement accounts, emergency funds, investments).

Some of your expenses are fixed. They're not going to change much over time or vary with the seasons. You probably know down to the penny your rent or mortgage payment as well as your car payment. You know what you spend on your various insurance policies. Some amounts come directly out of your paycheck, such as taxes, medical, and retirement, and are fixed as well.

With the fixed expenses in place, it's time to make decisions about the future. Now you can decide where you *need* to spend your money and where you can limit what you *want* to spend. The budgeting process can become fun right here; believe me. It gets exciting to see how relatively simple changes in your lifestyle and habits can dramatically influence the amount of money you can save. You must, of course, provide for your needs, but you have absolute control over your wants. You can ask your friends to help you with these decisions, or even ask a financial professional, but the ultimate choice rests in your hands. It's *your* financial future. You decide which *wants* move to the top of the list and which ones you're going to give up in favor of more important things. Small decisions can make a big impact. A four-dollar coffee each weekday is twenty dollars a week and more than $1,000 a year. Over ten years, that's more than $10,000—or the cost of a nice used car. It just got exciting, right? From coffee to a car!

Some people try to avoid the process of budgeting by using their bank account as the scorecard. Instead of accumulating their financial data, seeing where they are spending and making the needs-versus-wants decisions, they act based on the balance of their bank account. If there's money in there, they spend it. If not, they stop spending. The problem comes when unexpected expenses arrive.

When you budget, you know from the data that you spend about $600 a year on car repairs. You then set aside that amount in fifty-dollar monthly amounts. If you use your bank account as the budgeting mechanism and bring it down to zero at the end of every month, when the car breaks down you have a problem. Suddenly you can't drive, and you can't get to work without going into debt.

Continually monitor your spending. This is my third bit of advice when starting a budget. Gather and study the data monthly.

Ask yourself: What happened this month? Where did I meet my expectations? Where did I exceed them and what do I want to do differently next month? Should I make any big changes in my needs versus wants?

Don't let this topic seem intimidating. The essential point is to know how you're spending your money. You score big every time you make a wise purchase and keep yourself from spending unnecessarily. Sure, it may not be as fulfilling as winning an Olympic race, but watching your bank account grow due to your decisions can be quite satisfying.

THE SAVINGS GAP

Budgeting is a wealth enabler. The only way to create wealth is to spend less than you make. That means pushing your spending down as much as possible to create a greater spread between what you earn and what you spend—a savings gap. This is where money accumulates. You're either accumulating money or you're not. You're either spending less than you make or you're spending more. If you're spending less, you're saving. If you're spending more, you're going into debt. There is no middle ground.

I like the phrase, "live like a college student." It doesn't mean you have to eat ramen noodles all the time, but the mentality of living on as little as possible really works. The professional players who keep their college frugalness serve themselves well. I use this phrase with athletes because so many of them jump to a new stratosphere of living as soon as they gain newfound money and freedom.

The same thing can happen to you without realizing it. Let's say you get out of college, get your first job, and all of a sudden you find yourself in a really nice apartment, driving a nice car, and going on vacations. Your lifestyle suddenly matches your income or exceeds it. Or imagine you get a promotion and accompanying raise. You take the trip you've been wanting, and you move up to a nicer car. Suddenly, though, you're spending more than you make—leaving no savings surplus. In both scenarios, you have not created the savings you are seeking.

The goal is to increase the gap between your inflows and outflows. If inflows are greater than outflows you have a surplus; whereas if outflows are greater than inflows you have a deficit. You want the outcome where savings are generated because you spend less than you earn. The larger the "Savings Gap" between inflows and outflows, the more money is available for you to save and invest!

In America, the tendency is for people to spend 105 percent of what they make. You can't create savings and wealth spending 105 percent. Instead, you create a mountain of debt that grows larger every year no matter how much you earn. Consider, however, if you got the raise but kept your spending level or spent just slightly more. Your savings gap would grow very large over time. That's key. Instead of relying on risky investments to make money for you, you increase your wealth using budgeting and saving strategies with a much higher success rate.

REACH THE END ZONE BY SAVING

NFL pro Marshawn Lynch sometimes gets negative press for, well, not liking the press. But despite his past mistakes and his aloof conduct toward the media, his financial decisions seem to be strong.

Reportedly, he has made close to $50 million in his NFL career and hasn't spent much of it. He lives off money made from endorsements and other business ventures. You might struggle to call him thrifty since he makes more than $5 million from endorsement deals, but he definitely seems to understand the benefit of saving.

Saving is the byproduct of living on less than you earn. It is the financial strategy of retaining more of what you earn. Saving can be a very rewarding experience as you see your bank account grow in direct proportion to the daily decisions you make. If you cut out two coffees a week or skip going out to lunch, your bank balance immediately reinforces the positive behavior.

But once you've done the work of creating a savings surplus, you must defend your savings. Don't rationalize using it or dip into it for general living expenses. Develop the mindset that money deposited into a savings account is a one-way transaction toward a specific goal. It stays there until that goal is met or you have a wise plan for spending or investing some of it. Maybe you're saving for a new suit or Christmas presents for the kids or a larger expense like a house. Whatever your goals, defend your savings at all costs. Here are a few strategies that will help you do that:

- **The emergency fund**

  Every family should have six months of savings for emergencies. This is liquid money. It can be earning interest, but it's not invested. If the car breaks down, you can access the money that day. You don't have to sell stock or liquidate mutual funds; the money is sitting there ready for you. I suggest keeping the funds in a separate bank account and replenishing any money used as quickly as you can.

- **The power of compounding**

You probably understand now how small lifestyle changes can add up. Remember how the price of a cup of coffee a day added up to $10,000 in ten years? When saved, money starts to grow. The more you save, the more interest you earn. The power of compounding has huge exponential effects. You start to earn interest *on your interest*, savings *on top of savings*, creating a very large opportunity for increasing wealth. Once the ball is rolling, it gets bigger and bigger.

Here is an example of how a small amount of money grows due to compounding. The graph shows what would happen if twenty dollars was paid into an investment account each week over a thirty-year period and earned 4 percent interest.

The Power of Compounding

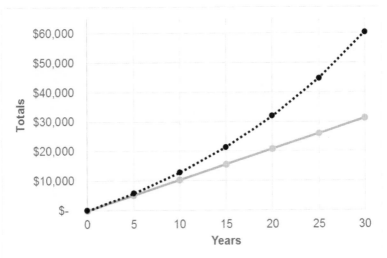

The bottom line represents the payments that were made, and the top line represents the sum of the payments made plus the interest earned. As you can see from the graph, in the early years there's not much of a gap between the two lines in the chart, because there's not much interest yet. However, over time, interest starts to accumulate and becomes quite meaningful. And a large part of the total balance in twenty, twenty-five and thirty years down the road is made up of interest. In fact, in this example, around the thirty-year mark, the interest component becomes greater than what was invested over the entire time.

Use the "Rule of 72" to see the power of compound interest. Take the number 72 and divide it by the whole number of your interest rate to see how long it takes that money to double. For example, if you're earning 4 percent, 72 divided by 4 tells you it will double in eighteen years. If you are earning 9 percent, dividing 72 by 9 tells you that your money will double within eight years. A $25,000 lump sum earning 9 percent would therefore double five times in a forty-year period, yielding $800,000. It also works the other way: if you're paying interest over 20 percent on a credit card, the amount will double within a three- to four-year period.

The Power of 72

Interest Rate	# of Years to Double
1%	72.0
2%	36.0
3%	24.0
4%	18.0
5%	14.4
6%	12.0
7%	10.3
8%	9.0
9%	8.0
10%	7.2
11%	6.5
12%	6.0
13%	5.5
14%	5.1
15%	4.8
16%	4.5
17%	4.2
18%	4.0
19%	3.8
20%	3.6

- **Youth advantage**

The earlier you start, the better. Unlike professional athletes who earn most of their money at the beginning of their careers, non-athletes usually earn increasingly more as their careers progress. If you keep your spending in check and create an ever-widening savings gap earlier in life, the power of compounding comes into play and you will see real gains in wealth.

Although starting earlier is ideal, it's never too late to implement these basic financial planning tenets. No matter your age and no matter what you've done in the past, you can start today. All the rules still apply, and today is better than tomorrow or not at all.

—— PLAYBOOK ——

RULE 2: BUDGET AND SAVE

KEY FUNDAMENTALS:
Create a budget
Increase your savings gap
Defend your savings

TAKE IT FROM A PRO

I won't be able to run, to compete in athletics, for the remainder of my life, so I have to have a plan to be comfortable in the later stages of my career.

I'm not a big spender anyways, but sometimes you have to remind yourself if something is a necessity.

Understand that you have to be patient. Focus on your craft and the money part of it will take care of itself.

- Kirani James, Olympic track gold and silver medalist (400 meters)

RULE 3

EDUCATE YOURSELF

UNDERSTAND YOUR NET WORTH SO YOU CAN IMPROVE IT OVER TIME

Money is vital to living. In modern society, you can't go a day without it. When you make money, you want it to last as long as you need it. Before you can make wise decisions, however, you need to understand how best to spend it, save it, and protect it.

Think about something you're good at—perhaps it's your profession, a hobby, or a sport. How did you get so good at it? You learned, you practiced, you watched other people do it. You improve in the areas where you spend time, money, and other resources.

Now think about money. You can improve in your financial decisions in the same way. Take time to educate yourself. Maybe you don't need to become an expert, but you want to know enough to be able to make your money work for you. **Your money can serve you; you don't have to serve your money.**

Growing up in Indiana, I idolized Larry Bird, Oscar Robertson, and Bobby Knight. I wanted to get better and better at basketball. In my hometown, I watched the best high school players and how hard they worked to improve. I emulated what they did and practiced all day during the summers. If I wasn't at the gym playing basketball, I was watching basketball, lifting weights, or exercising in some other way. I put in the time to get better, and I was fortunate to work my way into a college scholarship and successful pro career.

Take some initial steps to educate yourself and understand your finances before you call professionals to help you. By doing so, you'll be better prepared to lead your personal finance team.

I suggest you start with these three steps:
- Measure your personal finance acumen
- Understand your net worth
- Tackle your wealth weak spots (bad debts, unnecessary assets)

MEASURE YOUR PERSONAL FINANCE ACUMEN

Your acumen is your ability to make wise judgements or decisions in a particular setting. In finance, part of the learning process is understanding your starting point. What do you know and what do you still need to learn? Are you sitting on the bench, in the starting line-up, or an all-star when it comes to money? Anyone can improve his or her knowledge and capabilities.

Give yourself an honest evaluation about your understanding of money. When you have a realistic picture of where you are now, you can decide exactly where you want to go and how you will get there. Stop and consider the following statements:

I have a budget and stick to it each month.
I know how much debt I owe and have a plan for reducing it.

I know how much I spend and in what categories.

I know my net worth and I track the growth of my wealth.

I pay my credit card off in full each month.

I only buy things I can afford and do not spend lavishly.

I maintain an emergency fund in case unexpected costs arise.

I save regularly for my retirement.

I have a plan to grow in my career and increase my earnings potential.

I feel confident about my personal finances and having enough money to meet my goals.

Are you where you would like to be in each of these categories? If so, you're an all-star! Share your knowledge with others and keep learning. If you're not able to answer "yes" to the questions above, have no fear. You'll learn about each of these subjects and more in this book. Learning just a few fundamental rules about personal finance will lead to wiser choices. If where you are and where you want to be aren't the same, you know what you need to tackle.

UNDERSTAND YOUR NET WORTH

How much do you know about your finances? Do you really know how much you have in checking, savings, and retirement? Have you ever put your assets on paper? Once you understand your net worth, you can manage it and form a stronger strategy for financial growth.

It's part of educating yourself. You've worked hard to get where you are financially. You need to have financial data to be able to make decisions to improve your financial picture in the future. You have to know where you are before you can figure out where you're going.

Let's get a strategy going and put your net worth on paper. Then you can see your weak spots. You'll be able to answer questions that affect your financial situation: Do I have emergency funds? What do I owe? Do my debts have high-interest rates? (Refer to Rule 1 for a refresher on good debts and bad debts.)

When I teach college financial courses, I lead students to determine their personal net worth. This is a beneficial exercise as they put their financial story on a spreadsheet and see it clearly. For many, it's eye-opening and surprising. They enter the balances from their checking and saving accounts, investments, mutual funds, and assets (like personal property). Then they include their credit card debts, student loans, car payments, and other liabilities.

If their assets are greater than their liabilities, they see their positive net worth. Some who have a great deal of debt see a negative net worth. It becomes more real to them when they see it on paper or on the computer screen. When the reality of their financial situation is clear, they can plan for positive change.

Putting together a net worth statement can sound intimidating, but it's not. It's just a list of what you own (assets) and what you owe (liabilities) coupled with a little math. Let's do this together to come up with your net worth. We are going to look at what you have and what you owe.

Your assets are what you have. They include:

- Checking accounts
- Savings accounts
- Investment accounts (stocks, bonds, mutual funds)
- Individual Retirement Accounts
- Company 401(k) plans

- Educational accounts
- Car
- Boat
- Principal residence
- Investment property
- Personal property (furniture, jewelry, electronics, etc.)
- Business
- Other assets

Liabilities are what you owe. They include:

- Credit card debt
- Educational loans
- Car loans
- Home mortgages
- Other liabilities

I've shown an example here of what a net worth statement would look like for someone who owns a home, a couple of cars, and some retirement accounts, and has some loans.

Net Worth Example

Assets

Current Assets

Bank Account	Checking	5,000
Bank Account	Savings	12,000
Investment Account	Brokerage	
Investment Account	Mutual Funds	2,000
Other		
Other		

Tax-Advantaged Assets

Retirement Account	Company 401(k) Plan	45,000
Retirement Account	Individual Retirement Account (IRA)	5,500
Education Account	529 Plan	2,000
Other		
Other		

Personal Property

Real Estate	Principal Residence	225,000
Real Estate	Rental Property	
Personal Property	Automobile #1	20,000
Personal Property	Automobile #2	7,000
Personal Property	Boat, RV	
Personal Property	Furniture, Jewelry, Electronics, etc.	20,000
Real Estate	Rental Property	
Other		
Other		

Total Assets 343,500

Liabilities

Current Liabilities

Credit Card	Credit Card #1	9,000
Credit Card	Credit Card #2	
Pay-Day Loan		
Personal Loan		
Student Loan		27,000
Other		
Other		

Secured Loans

Mortgage	Principal Residence	205,000
Mortgage	Rental Property	
Home Equity Line of Credit	Principal Residence	
Auto Loan	Automobile #1	15,000
Auto Loan	Automobile #2	
Other		
Other		

Total Liabilities 256,000

Net Worth 87,500

As you can see from the example, assets are a big number at $343,500, but there's also more than quarter million dollars of debt. After subtracting the debt from the assets, there's a net worth of $87,500.

It's very important for you to complete a personal net worth assessment. Use the Net Worth worksheet available at TouchdownFinance.com. Take the time you need to find these numbers and get an accurate account of your net worth. Decisions you make moving forward will be based on this information.

Also consider an online program to easily monitor your net worth frequently. Your bank account and other accounts can feed into the program so it's always in real time. You just update the value of your assets like your home or your car. If you do the net worth statement in pencil or on a spreadsheet like the one I provide, you can easily create a new one periodically.

The net worth statement helps you see your decisions in action. If, for example, you save $10,000 over the course of a year, it will show up in the increase in your bank account balances. When you curb your expenditures as much as possible and increase your income over time, the gap between what you make and what you spend is wider and wider, causing your net worth to increase.

It's much easier to evaluate finances when you can see them on paper. It's an eye-opening experience. People say, "I had no idea my net worth was in six digits" or "I didn't realize I was negative." Negative is not necessarily a bad thing, depending on your stage of life. It's really a matter of where you go from here and what decisions you make, starting now.

Look at your net worth statement as frequently as you would look at your budget. Comparing this month's net worth statement to last month's tells you the direction you are heading and allows you to set goals. As the great baseball legend Yogi Berra said, "If you don't know where you're going, you'll end up someplace else."

Even if you don't have a huge savings gap and are just making regular payments on your car, mortgage, and educational loans, you will still see progress as the liabilities decrease. Even if your budget comes down to a zero at the end of the month, you could still be making positive steps by cutting down your liabilities.

A net worth statement is also very valuable for setting goals a month out, a quarter out, or years in the future. You can look where you've been and where you want to be, and plan how you're going to get there. You can see how money is going to be freed up, and you can allocate the savings in your asset column. If your statement shows car loans will be paid off in two years, what do you want to do with the money you were putting toward the car? Where will it do the most good? Where will it make the most impact?

Your net worth statement is different than your income. Your income might go up, but if your spending is rising at the same percentage or higher, your net worth won't increase, and your statement will reveal it. It shows what you really have, not what you make. Your net worth is always evolving based on your decisions. Higher income does not translate into higher net worth; higher income coupled with controlled expenses does.

TACKLE YOUR WEAK SPOTS

Once you see your financial story on paper, it's time to start analyzing it to identify the weak spots. Your goal is to make your net worth increase. Focus on these areas to improve your net worth:

- Tackle high-interest rate debt

- Knock out the urge to spend
- Game-plan big purchases

Tackle debt

It does not make sense to have money invested in a bank account making less than 1 percent if you have credit cards charging you more than 20 percent. Paying off high-interest debt is crucial. You receive an immediate return on your investment.

If you are relying on pay-day loans or high-interest credit cards to get by, then do everything possible to pay them off and/or switch to cards with a lower interest rate. When deciding which debt to pay off, be sure to make at least the minimum payments and then look to pay off the ones with the highest interest rates first. Lowering liabilities improves your net worth.

Knock out the urge to spend

Another big financial habit that can yield big results is to be content with what you have. Sure, it's a good mantra for living, but it also benefits you financially. If you're always buying the hottest cars, latest fashions, or newest tech gadgets, you will simply spend too much.

Former NBA star Antoine Walker went bankrupt even though he earned more than $100 million in his career. One of the many bad habits he had was acting on his obsession with cars. He once bought a Maybach for more than $400,000—the price of a nice house! He regrets that decision now, especially since he knows that once you drive a new car off the lot, the value goes down. He estimates that the car's value went down by $100,000 the moment he bought it. He sold it for much less than he paid for it.

Cars, like many things you buy, depreciate in value over time. Money does not lose its value. While I can't imagine a Maybach purchase ever being a wise financial move, we all need transportation, so we'll discuss the purchase of a car and how you can win financially in more detail in the next section.

Resisting the urge to spend is a great habit; so is delaying making purchases. Think about owning a $20,000 car for four years. That car would cost around $5,000 per year to own. Now consider if you could squeeze an extra two years out of that same car. Then that car's cost to own goes down to $3,333 per year. You pocket the savings and benefit from your thriftiness. If you pay off your car loan, use that money to pay other debt or direct it to savings. Don't immediately buy another car.

This principle is applicable to other assets listed in your net worth. Don't be in a rush to buy the newest things. Making do with what you own saves you money! Whether it's your furniture, electronics, clothes, jewelry, or other belongings, don't buy more. In fact, put some of it up for sale and use the proceeds to pay off debt. Many people have discovered how easy it is to sell personal belongings on eBay or similar sites.

Game-plan big purchases

When planning for a big purchase, put in the time and effort to ensure you are getting the best deal. I will use the purchase of a car as the example again because it's one of the biggest purchases that most of us make. And we buy cars several times in our lifetime. It's a purchase decision that many people get wrong.

I propose going through a rigorous process when making a large purchase. It starts by believing that the following equation is true:

More Knowledge = Better Solution + Better Deal

Said another way, the more you know, the higher the likelihood that you'll make the right choice at the right price.

Let's say you need a car and you're thinking of an SUV. More Knowledge is the initial research. You start by asking your friends what cars have given them good experiences. You scour the company website and test-drive cars. If you need to rent a car, you rent one of the cars you're considering buying. You can't beat that as a test-drive. You get to the point where your research starts to narrow your options.

Let's stop at this first step of the equation—More Knowledge—and see how the car buying process often plays out. Bob thinks, "I'd like a new car." He drives to the car dealership, takes a test-drive, picks out his favorite color, and takes his new car home. He doesn't know if this car is the best solution for him and his family, and he certainly has no idea if he got the better deal. He doesn't know how this car purchase will affect him financially.

What if Bob takes the time to gain knowledge about the car he needs and looks for a Better Solution? He separates his needs from his wants and doesn't buy more than he needs. He considers his family size. He researches mileage, longevity, dependability, and repairs. He reads buyer reviews of the car. He settles on the type of vehicle and the cost range he can afford. Now he can shop for the Better Deal.

Coupons, rebates, sales, and specials may be available if you seek them. If you're not satisfied (from your research) that you're getting the best deal, then walk away. There are plenty of other dealerships. A great negotiating technique is to tell the salesman you need to think about it overnight. Then leave. Come back and then ask for the deal you want. At that point, you're more likely to get a reduced price.

Even those of us who are very intentional about our finances may tend to skip one or even two steps in the equation. We may gain knowledge and jump to find the better deal without looking for other solutions. We may look for a great deal, but not on the thing that's targeted exactly to our needs. Sometimes the decision is so big, such as buying a first house or making a big investment, we get overwhelmed and don't adequately research the purchase. We shortcut the knowledge and solution steps because it's just too much to consider.

Life is a series of financial progressions. Give yourself permission to slow down and take the time to gather the information you need to engage in all three steps. You're never in such a hurry to act that you can't educate yourself. If anyone tells you that you must act *now*, consider that a red flag.

More Knowledge = Better Solution + Better Deal works for everything: financial planning, investments, purchases, even Christmas shopping. The more you know about the different options, the more often you will pick the best solution for you and get the better deal. Used over and over, this equation will allow you to become savvier. Each car deal will be easier and more intuitive, and the skills you gain will follow you as you confront future financial decisions. Financial education is a life-long activity. You'll always be learning and evolving. Changes abound. Situations require adjustments. The education you acquire for each decision will help you make better decisions more easily. In the next chapter, we'll talk about the financial professionals who can help educate and guide you.

—— PLAYBOOK ——

RULE 3: EDUCATE YOURSELF

KEY FUNDAMENTALS:
Measure your personal financial acumen
Understand your net worth
Tackle your weak spots

TAKE IT FROM A PRO

I think that being a point guard lends itself to being in control of a game. I have to understand where each player on the court likes the ball, what plays they like to run in the first quarter compared to the fourth quarter.

In finances, you have to trust your team and also stay aware of your day-to-day finances. Knowing what bill is going out when, what's going to work and what's not going to work. You have to invest in your own personal finances, as far as time. You have to be willing to keep track of things.

- Lindsay Whalen, Olympic gold medalist and Women's National Basketball Association (WNBA) champion

RULE 4

CONSULT ONLY TRUSTWORTHY PROFESSIONALS

BUILD A STRONG TEAM SO YOU CAN WIN WITH YOUR FINANCES

After 300-pound men have beaten on each other for three hours, the determining factor in a football victory is often a last-second field goal attempt. The camera zooms in on a smaller player off in the corner, usually wearing a jersey with the number three, kicking a football into a net. He then takes the field behind the massive line of nine of the 300-pound guys. The ball is hiked to a quarterback or punter who sets down the ball, and then a 180-pound hero kicks the football through the goalpost to make the winning field goal.

The coach has a good reason for sending in a smaller player at the most pivotal point in the game. This athlete is a kicking expert, a specialist. The coach isn't going to send out the biggest lineman to take the kick. He's going to bring out the guy who has devoted his entire life to kicking the football long and straight. No one has more practice and expertise, and this is exactly who needs to take the kick when the game is on the line.

The same is true of your financial life. You want people who devote their professional lives to their specialty to help you. **You want more than people who are technically qualified. You want the best people who can help you win financially.** Let's look at picking a strong financial team and how they can help you.

WHO ARE THE PLAYERS

Financial advisors fall into many categories, and it can get confusing. I'll try to make it easier to understand by identifying a few key players and what skills they'll bring to your financial team. Financial planners and advisors can play several of these roles, and the best ones will provide comprehensive services.

Financial planners

Financial planners look at your and/or your family's comprehensive financial situation and provide counsel on the entire plan. They analyze your current situation, talk to you about your goals, and then create a plan for you to reach your financial goals. They address many areas like budgeting, insurance, and retirement plans. Certified Financial Planner® (CFP®) is the highest and most respected designation in the field of planners.

Accountants

The primary relationship most individuals have with accountants is annual tax preparation. If you make money, you have to pay taxes, so a trusted accountant can be an integral part of your financial team. Accountants also help those with businesses or more complicated financial affairs. A strong accountant can also help you keep score of things like net worth, projections, and budgeting. Some accountants offer financial planning services. The top designation for accountants is Certified Public Accountant (CPA) with an additional designation for financial planner accountants as Personal Financial Specialists (PFS).

Insurance agents

Insurance agents help you find and purchase appropriate insurance, and you will need their services. Insurance is a form of financial protection that is often necessary. You want to shift the financial risk to insurance companies to absorb when it comes to health, auto, home, life, long-term care, and liability. For example, auto insurance covers your car as well as other cars, individuals, and property in the event you are involved in an accident. The potential costs of property damage and injuries can be incredibly expensive, and insurance covers those costs for you. In exchange, you pay relatively smaller sums in the form of premiums each year. You can do everything else right from an earning, savings, and investment standpoint, but one uninsured car accident or medical event can wipe it all out. Find an insurance agent who will make sure you and your family receive the right type of coverage so that you are protected.

Investment advisors, money managers, and brokers

When you have amassed enough money to begin to invest, you want to leverage the assistance of investment advisors and money managers. These types of professionals choose the investments for you based on your financial goals, time horizon, and risk profile. Brokers help their customers select, buy, and sell stocks and mutual funds. They are like other investment professionals, although primarily they make recommendations to their clients who make the final decision.

Attorneys

Attorneys can play a significant role in the financial advisory process, too. Lawyers can write wills, form trusts, and help with estate planning needs. They are useful not only to the very rich or in times of complicated legal matters. Everyone should have a will, and a trusted lawyer is the person to turn to.

CREDENTIALS MATTER

You want the most experienced and wisest financial advisor you can afford. Licenses, credentials, associations, and qualifications absolutely matter in this field. Financial professionals with lots of initials after their names have likely accomplished something to earn them. They've completed the education, training, and/or experience to earn credentials.

Those qualifications, which often give them an edge over competitors, are a differentiator that adds credibility and demonstrates experience. That experience is invaluable. It has allowed them to learn from both the good decisions they've helped their clients make and the bad decisions they've seen out in the real world. Experienced professionals understand what can go wrong. They've seen how an illness or disability affects a family. They know what a death can mean for those without life insurance. They have clients who have lost their jobs. You can trust them to guide you through the financial implications of negative experiences.

The more credentialed advisors also have more at stake. Many go through a background check and are fingerprinted. They must attend educational courses each year, and generally are required to carry malpractice insurance. If something were to go wrong, you have recourse for recovery.

We've seen this play out with professional athletes. Former NFL cornerback Asante Samuel filed an arbitration claim against Morgan Stanley and Wells Fargo Advisors when they failed to supervise one of their financial advisors (who had gone from the first firm to the second). Samuel and another defendant claimed the advisor invested their money without their knowledge. The companies chose to settle with a combined settlement of more than $2 million. Just as in medicine or law, professional liability insurance may be in place to compensate you if a financial advisor does not live up to professional standards.

Here are some abbreviations you'll commonly see when researching financial advisors and what they mean:

CFP®—Certified Financial Planner

To obtain the CFP® designation, these professionals demonstrate experience, take additional educational courses, and pass rigorous testing.

CPA—Certified Public Accountant

This is the highest designation in the accounting industry. This designation means the accountant has passed stringent educational and experience requirements followed by a very difficult set of tests.

AIF—Accredited Investment Fiduciary

When you see these letters, you can know that someone has been tested and can help clients choose wise investments.

PFS—Personal Financial Specialist

This is a designation for accountants who practice in financial advisory. This designation also denotes experience, qualifications, and continued education. It's what you should look for if you want an accountant to help with more than your taxes.

CFA—Certified Financial Analyst

CFAs are specialists in investment opportunities. They may also serve as investment advisors and money managers, because they analyze the financial records of corporations and investments on a very deep level.

CLU—Chartered Life Underwriter

CLU is the highest designation in the life insurance industry. Advisors with a CLU are experts in life insurance and understand the different products offered.

All these credentials can be verified. You can check with the licensing organization to make sure the professional you are considering for your team is still active and permitted to practice.

Also, each state will license their professionals, and you can verify they are active and in good standing. Some professionals hold a license given by the Financial Industry Regulatory Authority (FINRA), the regulatory authority for registered investment professionals with securities licenses. You can get a detailed report on the licenses they have, where they have worked, and how long they've been in the industry, plus any criminal convictions or civil judgements, arbitration awards, or disciplinary action through FINRA Broker Check at brokercheck.FINRA.org.

FOLLOW THE MONEY

Professionals earn their compensation in different ways. For budgeting purposes, it will be helpful to know how they make money.

Commission: One of the primary methods of compensation is commission. Commission-based professionals are paid a percentage or fee based on the transaction. Insurance and annuities are generally commission-based. As the client, you do not pay fees out of your pocket; they are paid by the company you buy the product from. For example, if you buy an auto insurance policy, you pay the premium price to the company, who pays the insurance agent behind the scenes.

Asset-based fees: Professionals can also be compensated by asset-based fees. For example, you pay people who manage your money a percentage of the money they are managing. They make more money when you make more money. As the level of your holdings increase, their fees rise, too.

Project or hourly fees: Another way professionals make money is project or hourly fees. The flat fee or hourly rate is negotiated up front and the professional delivers the work to you in exchange for the fee. Larger projects take more of the professional's time and cost more. You'll find that accountants and financial planners often charge project or hourly fees for services such as preparing tax returns or developing a financial plan.

When you consider hiring a professional, know how they are compensated and consider how that might affect the advice they give. For example, if you consult with a life insurance agent and buy a policy through Prudential, Prudential pays the life insurance agent. You want to be sure the life insurance agent has presented the best product to you, not the one that is most lucrative to the agent. Ask to see a comparison of the products researched.

One other consideration related to compensation is the pool of products a professional has to choose from. Some professionals are "captive." This means they work for a particular company and can only sell their products. An example is a State Farm Insurance office. If you go into a State Farm office, they will offer you State Farm products.

Other professionals are independent brokers. They can access the products of many different companies. They look at the problem you're trying to solve, such as choosing the best car insurance. They might recommend Progressive, Hartford, MetLife, or another company's product depending on which is the best fit and most economical. Some captive agents are also able to shop around for products from other companies, but that's usually reserved for independent agents.

DRAFTING YOUR TEAMMATES

NBA superstar Kevin Durant received a lot of criticism in 2016 after deciding to leave the Oklahoma City Thunder and join the Golden State Warriors. The move stunned the basketball world because it matched arguably one of the best players with arguably the best team in the world. As most predicted, the Warriors did win the 2017 NBA Championship, and Durant was awarded the Most Valuable Player trophy in the finals.

When it comes to picking teams, think about your criteria. Would you pick the best teammates, or would you just take whoever you could, no matter the skill level? My vote would be to assemble the best team possible. If I get to choose, I want to be surrounded by proven winners!

Once you know what *type* of professionals you want on your team, it's time to find them. Ask friends and family whom they recommend and why. Reach out to your current advisors. Your tax accountant may be able to give you a good referral for an auto insurance agent. If you're looking for a certified financial planner, you might be able to get a good referral from other professionals who work for you.

Once you get referrals that look promising, verify their licenses and credentials with the licensing agencies and your state. Watchdog organizations, like FINRA and the Better Business Bureau, can be very helpful, as well as online sites where clients rate their experience with individual professionals.

Once you are comfortable with the licenses and credentials, meet the agent and see if your outlook and personalities are a match. Even among high-level professionals, you want a good fit—someone with whom you feel comfortable talking and discussing matters as personal as finances. You'll discover that some advisors are better suited for working with certain wage-earning brackets, stages of career, or age groups. Some professionals are community-based, and some are urban. The key is understanding what you need, finding the professional who is best suited to meet that need, and making sure you are a fit.

In the end, you want someone with whom you are comfortable. Personalities do matter, and a good match helps increase the chances of success. You may want to choose someone who will push you in new directions. For example, when I was choosing my college, I wanted to play for the best academic NCAA school that would give me a scholarship. The second set of criteria was that I wanted a coach with whom I felt comfortable and who would help me become successful. Location was not as important.

I chose Butler University, which happened to be the closest Division 1 school to my home. The clincher was when I met the head coach, coaching staff, and players on my recruiting trip. I felt comfortable with them from day one, and the small school atmosphere fit my personality. I appreciated the geniality and the compassion of the folks around me. It was fully evident that this was where I wanted to spend my college years. You want this same feeling with your financial team.

Here is a list of categories you will want to cover when interviewing potential advisors:

Years of experience

Education

Certificates, licenses, and accreditations

Products and services offered

Style, philosophy, and values

References and client testimonials

Industry ratings and regulators (BBB, FINRA)

Fee structure

Other reasons they want to serve you

YOU'RE THE QUARTERBACK

Your money is one of the most important aspects of your life. You want somebody you trust who is going to give you the advice you *need* to hear even when you may not *want* to hear it. You want someone who will do the best for you even if it's difficult. When you think about coaches, the best ones aren't necessarily those you like the most. The strongest are the ones who make you and the team better players. Look for people who will coach you. You want to learn from them. These are paid professionals. Their job is to teach you about the products and the solutions and to help you understand the advice they are giving. You should ask questions and be encouraged to do so. That's how you learn and become more effective.

Tom Brady is an incredible quarterback and surely will be enshrined in the Pro Football Hall of Fame once his career has ended. No one doubts his influence on the New England Patriots nor his contribution to the team's numerous Super Bowl victories in the past fifteen years. However, arguably, coach Bill Belichick has been more instrumental in the team's ability to play at a high level during that time period.

Love him or hate him, since 2010 Belichick-coached teams have won approximately 75 percent of their NFL games. That's an incredible average! His philosophy for his teams is simple, yet decisive and powerful. His mantra for his players is just "do your job." He finds disciplined players, trusts them to do their jobs, and teaches them to trust their teammates to do their jobs as well. You should not expect Super Bowl success with your personal finances, but you should not minimize the importance of your team, either.

When you're considering which type of professional and which specific people you are going to put on your team, remember you're the boss. It's your money. You want to be educated and understand the recommendations of your team of financial advisors so you know when to defer to their advice or follow your own wisdom. You have the right to pick who you want on your team and can hire and fire as you see fit. You don't want to be fickle with financial advisors, but you do want to make sure that you have people you trust, who are working hard and getting good results. Using these principles, you can build a team that will help you move toward financial success.

—— PLAYBOOK ——

RULE 4: CONSULT ONLY TRUSTWORTHY ADVISORS

KEY FUNDAMENTALS:
Select advisors carefully
Study their credentials
Lead your financial team

TAKE IT FROM A PRO

As a field goal kicker, if I don't have a good team around me, it would be hard for me to be successful. I have a lot of faith and trust in those guys who are in front of me and block for me. I don't necessarily know what those linemen are supposed to be doing on every single play, but I know that I trust them to do their job. I know that they know what they're doing.

The same goes for my financial team. I trust them to know what they are doing. That's what makes a good team. Surround yourself with good people and build that trust over time.

- Graham Gano, National Football League (NFL) All-Pro kicker

RULE 5

PROTECT YOUR ASSETS

GUARD YOURSELF FROM MISTAKES THAT CAN CAUSE FINANCIAL DISASTER

A more appropriate name for this chapter might be "Just Say No." Just getting used to the word "no," even said to yourself, could save you considerable headache and will certainly save you money. We've talked earlier in this book about taking things slowly—not rushing into buying expensive things and taking time to make wise financial decisions.

For some, it's easier to tell themselves no than to say it to others. One former NFL pro told me that during rookie training, a trainer told the guys to think of one family member who isn't afraid to tell people no. He advised the athletes to send people seeking their money to that family member. This former pro's dad took on this role for him. The son and dad had an understanding: Dad would listen politely to solicitors, but the answer would be no.

Regardless of how much money you have, you might find yourself in a similar place, or at least able to relate to the need to protect your money and its potential to grow. I've seen the same few mistakes played out over and over in people's lives. By avoiding these mistakes, you can keep the money you have and use it to ensure a comfortable future.

If you have a little or a lot, it's worth protecting. You've worked hard for what you have, so let me point out these mistakes in the hope that you won't make them. Mistakes can be wealth killers. Keep these tips in mind to protect yourself and your assets:

Wait to select a mate.

Don't be too generous with loans and gifts.

Insure yourself properly.

Defend your credit score.

WAIT TO SELECT A MATE

This seems very personal. I get that. The truth is that money is also very personal, and entering a bad relationship or the responsibility of parenthood before you're ready can be devastating. I'm not trying to stick my nose into your personal business, but I do want you to consider this topic carefully. Some of you have probably already made this mistake. I know I have.

Today I'm a happily married man with four children, so this is a topic dear to my heart. I wish I had listened to advice like this when I was in my twenties. During those years, I went through a nasty divorce and dealt personally with child support obligations. The divorce was not only emotionally painful, it was expensive, and much of my net worth evaporated. My son was God's gift in the middle of the mess. And although that marriage produced this wonderful son who's now in the US Marines, my decisions in early adulthood were costly to me. It took two and a half very expensive years to finalize the divorce, and then I faced yearly custody battles.

Of course, I probably wouldn't have listened to this advice back then, but I wish I had understood how financially damaging rushing into relationships can be. I know a former pro athlete who had to buy his house four times! He bought it the first time, then he had to buy it back in divorce settlements with two ex-wives, and finally he refinanced it to avoid foreclosure.

Make life-changing decisions wisely, especially marriage. It's staggering that half of all marriages end in divorce. Financially, divorce takes away, in most cases, at least half of one's net worth. Divorces can be financially devastating. Also understand that having children, planned or unplanned, will be costly and should be budgeted for appropriately. Good relationships are worth the expense, but bad ones can be costly. Weddings are expensive, kids are expensive, but divorce is even more expensive. That's why divorce lawyers have fancy billboards and slick websites.

To understand the financial significance of some life-changing decisions, keep this in mind:

Cost of an average wedding—$35,000

Cost to raise a child—$230,000; $13,000/year (birth to age 18)

Divorce attorneys—$15,000-$30,000

Average child support—$5,000/year

Depending on your state, the divorce could cost even more. In a divorce, you divide assets. A working spouse may have to pay a non-working spouse alimony. Child support is paid to the custodial parent. It costs everyone involved a lot more than money. These choices cost BIG and hurt more than your pocketbook.

NBA All-Star player Dwight Howard learned his lesson in this regard and is paying for it financially. To date, Howard has fathered five children with five different women, all while in his twenties. Sure, he loves his kids, but Howard admits he should have been more responsible.

Howard's wealth should be able to handle the child support obligations, but it would have been better if he had waited to raise a family until he was more mature and his life was more stable. Athletes live in a whirlwind of travel and demanding schedules. Many of them experience the strongest relationships when they are out of the limelight. Consider what you have going on in your life. Be ready to focus on marriage or on being a great mom or dad when the time is right.

Before I end this section, I want to address prenuptial agreements, though I know this is also highly personal and can be divisive. Here's what I advise: a prenuptial agreement might be necessary to bring peace of mind. If both parties are in favor, then it might bring more peace than disruption. Discussions about this before marriage can also be useful to reveal important issues like family dynamics and commitments. Depending on your finances, protecting your assets might be necessary, and this agreement can be entered into harmoniously by both spouses. Unfortunately, the prenup discussion often reveals some ulterior motives in some professional athletes' relationships, so it is a good thing to discuss before the wedding. It's not a "have to" but might be worth considering.

When you find the right person and start a family, the money you spend will be worth it. But until then, just say no or at least "wait." Marriage and parenthood are life-changing decisions and will be blessings when treated with the maturity, time, and attention they deserve.

DON'T BE TOO GENEROUS WITH LOANS AND GIFTS

Speaking of family dynamics, be cautious when loaning money to family members and friends. I must include this tip because far too often the loans are not paid back. Highly paid professional athletes often face this when they come into money quickly, and when men and women go pro, their salaries become public knowledge. Then the pressure to help others intensifies.

You may face this too, even if you don't have a lot of money. If you're wise and follow the rules of this book, and your money grows, you might be faced with family members or friends wanting a part of it. Here's what I say about that: take care of people, of course, but be reasonable.

As a rule, don't loan more money than you can afford to give. You might get it back, but you might not. A loan shouldn't damage your financial situation or alter your goals. Whether friends need help out of a financial struggle or they have an investment opportunity for you, be careful, wise, and informed before parting with your money. So many loans go unpaid that you have to be prepared for this possibility.

If you do choose to loan money, always have an official promissory note. This should include both signatures, the sum you intend to loan, a specific date when it will be paid back, and the rate of interest. Stay in control of your money and the loan process.

Large monetary gifts can also be a mistake in some circumstances. You might give someone money with a genuine spirit of generosity, but beware that doing so could cause harm and strain relationships.

One former retired NFL athlete told me that during his rookie year he bought his mother and his grandmother homes. He was happy to be able to do this for them. Later he bought his in-laws a home. It gave him joy to be that generous. One day, however, his mom gave him a stack of unpaid bills. She expected him to also pay the property taxes, utility bills, and maintenance costs on the house he gifted. He didn't consider that his gift was going to turn into a permanent responsibility for all costs associated with the house. Family members came to expect and even depend on his money. Long after his NFL career ended, the family still expected to maintain the lifestyle he established for them. Unfortunately, the relationship with family members became strained.

"Be careful," he told me as a warning to others. "Just be mindful that whatever you introduce them to, the expectations still exist through all your playing days and thereafter," he said. Most of us don't have the resources to buy homes for all our relatives. I get that. But this is an example of how a good gesture can alter the relationship between family members. If you send a niece one hundred dollars every year on her birthday, but then face a time when you cannot afford that, will she be disappointed? Are gifts from you expected regularly? Consider the relationships and the expectations your gifts may bring. Be generous and loving in a way that won't hurt you financially or cause rifts in relationships.

While we're talking about generosity, let me mention giving to trusted charities and non-profits you care about. This is different from overly generous gifts to family members or friends. Being a cheerful, even sacrificial, giver has many positive benefits. Even small gifts can make a big difference to charitable organizations. Consider giving regularly to your church, disaster relief, or a social cause you care about. These gifts can affect many people and are usually tax deductible.

It's OK to take care of people and organizations that you love. Include them in your plans and budgets. Be cautious, however, when others ask for money. Stop and think it through. Make sure you can afford it.

INSURE YOURSELF PROPERLY

Insurance seems costly, and it is, but a disaster without it could cause greater financial harm. Having adequate insurance can lessen the blow for you and those you love. Let's look at some of the big types of insurance and what they protect.

Type	Typical Cost	Intended Use	Consequences of Not Having It Or Not Enough
Life	$300/year for a $250,000 20-year Term Life policy for a healthy individual	Provides financial means for surviving family members to pay for the funeral, cover the deceased's debts, satisfy tax obligations, and have money to live on.	Families can be left devastated financially when the main breadwinner passes away.
Home	$300-$1,000/year depending on where you live and value of the home	Reimburses homeowner for damages caused by fire, storms, or other unforeseen events.	Few people have the financial means to rebuild their homes if destroyed.
Auto	Annual premiums vary widely, depending on driver's age, accident history, credit score, and type of car, with the average policy costing $800/year	Required in many states and covers the costs of auto repairs, medical expenses, liabilities, and other damages sustained from auto accidents.	Accidents can cause extensive property and auto damage and medical costs can be very expensive for the occupants of the vehicles.
Medical	Costs vary widely depending on family size, state of residence, and income levels, with average family policy costs at more than $10,000/year	Pays for healthcare and medical bills.	Serious illnesses and injuries can cost in the millions and wipe out a family's wealth.
Disability	$500/year for $30,000 annual coverage	Replaces a portion of the income lost when an employee is unable to perform a job because of illness or injury.	Families can be left devastated financially when the main breadwinner is unable to earn a living.

Defend your credit score

Another critical piece of your personal financial future is your credit score. Credit scores are numerical grades given to you based on your creditworthiness. They change over time based on many factors in your credit history. The scores range from 300 to 850 and are statistically derived and tracked by three primary credit bureaus.

Category	Range
Excellent	750-850
Good	700-749
Fair	650-699
Poor	550-649
Bad	300-550

Credit Bureaus

Equifax

Experian

TransUnion

Your credit score is important because it is what lenders consider when deciding whether to loan you money. It is used by companies deciding to grant you credit cards, car loans, home loans, etc. You could get denied credit if your score is low, or you could have to pay a lot more in interest compared to someone with a high credit rating. Here's a list of factors that go into your score:

Paying your bills on time

Having a successful history of repaying loans

Being granted credit, but not using all of it

Having a mix of different types of loans

Not applying for too many loans, nor having too few

Monitoring your credit report and fixing problems

Credit scores are a big factor in your ability to buy cars and homes. They also affect your being approved for credit cards and even renting apartments and applying for some jobs. Take the necessary steps to keep your score as high as you can. You can access your credit reports for free once a year from each of the three credit bureaus. Visit the site www.annualcreditreport.com to get your free annual reports. I encourage you to check your score!

Protecting your assets is more about maintaining good habits and making wise decisions than it is about doing anything overly complicated. Avoid costly mistakes by just saying no. This will lead to success. Ignore these tips and you might wreck your financial life. You can protect what you have, defend against making wealth-killing mistakes, and avoid falling into these common traps.

—— PLAYBOOK ——

RULE 5: PROTECT YOUR ASSETS

KEY FUNDAMENTALS:
Wait to select a mate
Don't be too generous
Insure yourself properly
Defend your credit score

TAKE IT FROM A PRO

When you're young, you don't really worry about injuries or things that can happen to you in the future. It was later on in my career that I said, "How do I take care of myself? How do I prepare and protect myself?"

I feel like now I have an understanding about where I want to be financially and how to invest and protect my money. I know how I want to spend money. I rely on the way I was raised and what my family taught me and how my advisors help me.

- Ian Mahinmi, National Basketball Association (NBA) world champion

RULE 6

PLAN YOUR FUTURE

CREATE WEALTH FOR THE LONG TERM

We all have to plan for the future—it's imperative if we want to live comfortably for the rest of our lives. But it's magnified for professional athletes I serve because their playing careers are relatively short. You've probably heard the joke that NFL translates "Not For Long." Injuries in football are commonplace and bring about sudden, early retirements. I counsel athletes to think about how they will earn money when their professional sports careers are over. They have to plan for the time their income will drop off in a big way.

Thankfully, the rest of us don't have to worry about a 275-pound defensive end finishing our professional careers with one brutal hit. You may be able to stay in the same job, remain in the same industry, or work for the same company your whole career, which could span forty-to-fifty years. A registered nurse, for example, might work at several different hospitals or clinics during a career, but he or she could realistically remain a nurse until retirement.

The importance of the career path you choose cannot be understated. Your career, and the efforts you exert to get there, will directly impact your ability to create wealth. **Plan for the earnings potential that you want, be realistic about what you can attain, and then make it happen.** Your career is the driver of your top line, your earnings, and your income—and what you then can preserve and put toward your future by making good financial decisions.

Your ultimate career path is instrumental to your creation of wealth. The steps to achieving your career goals are equally as important. Let's look at how you can plan your financial future through these three areas of focus:

Furthering your education
Winning at what you do
Planning for a rich retirement

FURTHER YOUR EDUCATION

I was blessed to have grown up in a family of educators. My mom was an elementary school principal, and my dad was an assistant principal at a high school. I never considered *not* going to college. For one thing, I was eager to play college basketball. More importantly, my parents pounded into my head that a college education was an absolute must. Their influence launched my desire to keep learning and learning. Even after spending almost half of my life in school, I still am eager to learn.

I understand why "further your education" was such good advice. Now, I was extremely lucky to have an incredible college experience at Butler University. I learned a lot in the classroom and absorbed knowledge, skills, and tools that I get to use in my everyday work. But it was also a unique environment where I could mature as a young adult, interact with people from all over the United States and the world, and learn how to learn. Most of my closest friendships today began in college.

But there's a financial element to a college education that is profound. According to The Common Application (2017), "someone with a college degree will earn $1 million more than someone with a high school diploma." In most cases, lifetime earnings are more for those who have advanced degrees.

Someone with a bachelor's degree will earn 77 percent more than someone with a high school diploma. A master's degree holder is likely to earn twice that of a high school graduate. Another recommended path to education is a two-year trade or vocational school that teaches skills related to a specific job. Career earnings for trade school graduates are in the $1.8 million range on average, similar to someone with an associate degree.

It's never too late to get an education. There are innovative ways for adult learners to further their education, no matter their personal circumstances. I am a testament that you *can* teach an old dog new tricks! I know, because I was still working toward degrees in my forties, while balancing a full-time job and raising a family. It can be done.

Universities are using technology to bring solid education in non-traditional ways. Gone are the days when you have to physically go to a college campus to receive your education. Yes, you can still attend classes in person, and some students prefer to learn in that atmosphere. However, the online learning experience has improved dramatically and has been tailored to fit the needs of adult learners.

You don't have to press pause on your life to go back to school. I joke that my doctorate was obtained with the assistance of Eric Cartman. He's a main character in the animated series *South Park*.

My time to study was after work, after dinner, and after my wife and kids went to bed. I usually started schoolwork at ten o'clock, ending a few hours later. That happened to be when *South Park* episodes were playing on *Comedy Central.* Laughing at Eric and the characters in the show kept me awake.

Continuing your education is a wise path to financial success and should be considered at any stage of your life or career. Further education might increase your earnings potential, and, thus, your wealth and financial security.

WIN AT WHAT YOU DO

While you're working, wherever you're working, whatever you're doing, do your best. This good advice also happens to be biblical! Colossians 3:23 (NIV) commands: "Whatever you do, work at it with all your heart, as working for the Lord." The verse is pretty clear. Now let's explore what this means for you and your career and how it relates to your personal finances.

Here's how the workplace views it: the better you do, the more you will advance in an organization, and the more you will get paid. We see this vividly in professional sports, since the salaries that players earn are public information. Stephen Curry and Lebron James were projected to earn more than $33 million during the 2017-2018 NBA season. Yes, those are astronomical salaries and those numbers are reserved for the elite professional athletes. However, Curry and James are arguably two of the best basketball players in the world, and they should earn more than the rest of the players in the league. Their employers feel they are worth those salaries, and many teams would love to be able to have them on their teams, even at that price.

Every job or industry has different educational prerequisites and requirements. The US Bureau of Labor Statistics publishes its *Occupational Outlook Handbook,* an interesting resource listing careers, what's required for the job, education and certifications, salary expectations, outlook for the industry, and other information.

Let's take a look at a small sample of various occupations, the annual earnings potential of each, and what you need to do or have in order to succeed:

Accountant	$60,000	Attend college, earn a CPA certification/license
Carpenter	$45,000	Attend a trade school, serve an apprenticeship
College professor	$80,000	Attend college, obtain advanced degree
Construction worker	$32,000	On-the-job training
Doctor	$200,000	Attend college and medical school, serve in an internship or residency program
High school teacher	$58,000	Attend college, obtain teaching license

Mechanic	$38,000	Attend a vocational school, gain industry certification
Professional athlete	$1 million +	Possess incredible athletic ability and talent in a particular sport, play well
Registered nurse	$70,000	Attend college, gain practical experience

Source: Bureau of Labor Statistics. (2017). *Occupational Outlook Handbook*. Retrieved from https://www.bls.gov/ooh/

Unfortunately, not all of us can pick the highest paying job and expect everything will fall into place. We all have different talents, skills, and passions. The choice of occupation may be limited to our physical, emotional, or mental abilities. We may have family to take care of and cannot afford to go to school for many years, as some occupations require.

The key is to choose an occupation wisely and then make the most of it. Your job is your greatest source of income and creator of wealth over time. Be willing to put time and effort into your work, stay at the top of your game, and make "halftime" adjustments as needed. Let's discuss these ways to "win at what you do" in more detail.

Give maximum effort. Be willing to put in the time and effort to advance in your career. I started my accounting career in the international tax office of a Big 4 accounting firm, Price Waterhouse. I experienced the usual career progression as a tax professional.

It usually takes two-to-three years as a junior entry-level accountant before you can advance to a senior accountant. Depending on how you do there, you can advance in two-to-three years to the assistant manager level. From assistant manager, you can become a manager after another two-to-three years, and then the next steps are director, and then partner. The progression is pretty standard. You know that if you do well, you'll probably move up the ladder.

Each step along the way takes time, and you encounter different types of challenges at each stage. You don't have to be a workaholic who neglects family and friends to move ahead in your career and enhance your earnings potential. It takes time in accounting to gain experience with the technical aspects of the profession, with training and managing people, and with leveraging technology to move ahead. Someone who isn't willing to pay their dues and work for the opportunities might miss them completely. Most people don't become boss overnight, especially in an industry like accounting where you can't learn many of the skills until you actually have the opportunity to do them hands-on. A few of us will be stars and advance more quickly than others, but we all have to pay our dues and earn our way.

Stay at the top of your game. We have discussed the fact that credentials, licenses, and accreditations matter. In the same way that you want the most experienced and wisest financial advisor you can afford on your team, your company wants the best employees. Staying at the top of your game entails that you make the effort to keep improving your skill sets so you stay as marketable and valuable as possible.

Online information is readily accessible, even from our phones. Read the latest articles or blogs from the experts. If you're in education, know about the latest teaching trends or opportunities. Staying current in your industry will help you set yourself apart from your peers. Different occupations have different opportunities for personal and professional growth. Seek out ways to expand your knowledge and work on your resume.

Evaluate your strengths and your weaknesses. What are your greatest assets as an employee? What are your liabilities, and where can you improve to make yourself more marketable? What skills would set you apart from your colleagues? What skills are you lacking?

You'll also benefit by seeking the counsel of others. Experienced folks in your profession or industry may welcome the opportunity to mentor you. Don't be afraid to ask, "How did you become successful?" I love the mantra that Marshall Goldsmith (2013) described in his leadership writings about the process "ask, learn, follow up, and grow." Even though he was challenging leaders, his thoughts can apply to any employee. He challenged people to keep learning and growing; if not, you'll become obsolete in the twenty-first century.

Professional athletes spend their off-seasons with personal trainers and position coaches to get better at what they do. You don't have to spend your Saturdays lifting weights and running up hills, but it's a good idea to keep sharpening your job skills.

Have a back-up game plan. I don't mean to contradict my previous statements, but it's wise to think about what else you can do to make money if your career stalls or is suddenly cut short, or if you simply want to do something else. You might have to make a half-time adjustment.

WNBA star Lindsay Whalen says she goes into every game with a primary game plan but also a plan B, C, and D. "You hope that things work with your first game plan, but sometimes you have to go to those other options. Between our head coach, the other coaches, and me, it's always fun to figure out those challenges and try to make it work for each game."

Thousands of parents have told their kids with pro sports dreams, "Get your education so you have something to fall back on." No parent wants to squash their kids' dreams, but it's good to face reality and be prepared for all circumstances. Keep your network alive and be active in associations, societies, and affiliations in your profession and industry. Optimize your career now so it works for you later.

Technological changes may force you to retool your skill set or even change occupations. Your skill set might translate into an industry that you've not thought about before. One evening class at a community college might spark some ideas for a new career path. Whatever your job is now, or even if you're job-hunting, give it your best, but don't stop dreaming about the career you really want. It is never too late to change course.

Winning at what you do means doing everything you can to put yourself in the best position possible to earn a good living. A common theme among successful people is effort. Doing your best will help you win and lead you to financial success and wealth.

PLAN FOR A RICH RETIREMENT

During your working career, you are in the financial accumulation phase of your life. You're making money and hopefully saving money for the future. You should also be planning for the future years when you're not able to work as much or just want to relax and enjoy retirement. We work hard now so we don't have to one day, right?

With today's life expectancy increasing, someone who stops working at age sixty-five might have more than twenty years of needing income in the senior adult years. US Social Security will hopefully be there when we retire, but it's not guaranteed, and the projections for the Social Security trust fund are not exactly encouraging. Corporate pensions have decreased substantially over the past decades, and now very few employers offer defined benefit pension plans for workers.

You have to put some thought into your retirement and take responsibility for saving in order to take care of yourself and your family. The risk of not saving enough for retirement is just too great. Without adequate retirement savings, you might have to continue working longer than expected, decrease your standard of living, or even sell your home or possessions that you've worked hard for. Let's look at a typical life cycle of your wealth.

During your working years, you are accumulating wealth and increasing your net worth. In the chart below, the tip of the line would be your "nest egg," or the culmination of what you've saved over your working lifetime, preparing for retirement. Once you stop working and begin retirement, then you're in the spend-down phase, and your wealth will decrease, as more money is going out than coming in.

Wealth Life Cycle

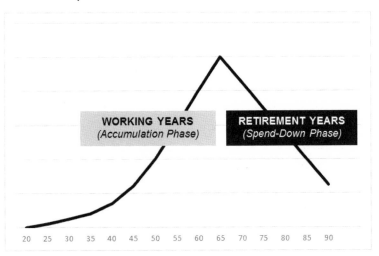

You don't know how long you will live, so it's crucial that you don't spend too much in your earlier years of retirement. You want your money to last your lifetime. You don't want to be in a situation where you haven't saved enough early on in your career or spent too much once retired.

Here's the good news: you've got choices of many types of retirement savings opportunities, no matter your age or how much money you make. The government even has tax incentives for those saving for retirement. The money you set aside in retirement accounts, like a 401(k) or Individual Retirement Account (IRA), is deducted from your taxable income, so it's not taxed, and the earnings on that money isn't taxed then either. That money can grow without being taxed until you begin to use it. By allowing compounding to work for you in a tax-advantaged and tax-deferred way, large sums can be accumulated over time. It's worth investing in these types of plans. You'll pay taxes eventually, but by the time you'll need that money you'll probably be earning less, you'll be in a lower tax bracket, and the taxes will be much smaller.

Some insurance products, like annuities and life insurance, can also be quite useful for building up your savings. The money you invest will escape taxation during your higher-earning years. The earnings are tax-advantaged as you defer paying any tax until retirement, like a 401(k). Another reason these products are appealing is that they shift the risk of how long you may live to the insurance company. For example, if you have an annuity that pays a certain amount every month for life, then you are guaranteed that money each month, no matter how long you live. If you have life insurance and something should happen to you, your family is protected from the financial hardship of you not being there.

You can create wealth for your long-term financial well-being. The decisions you make about your education and career play a role in your ability to live the way you want once retired. You can adjust if you are not on the track you want; it's never too late to change course toward a secure financial future.

—— PLAYBOOK ——

RULE 6: PLAN YOUR FUTURE

KEY FUNDAMENTALS:
Further your education
Win at what you do
Plan for a comfortable retirement

TAKE IT FROM A PRO

I was always overthinking, to a point, what am I going to do next? What am I passionate about? Do I want to just continue in the sport of soccer? Ever since my rookie season, I had always been planning and thinking and preparing for a transition time, which is where I am now.

Sharpening your skills and performing at a high level transfers to the real world. I'll continue to sharpen my skills and perform at a high level to show the quality I can bring to financial planning.

- Brian Carroll, Major League Soccer (MLS) (2003-2017)

RULE 7

STICK TO SAFE INVESTMENTS

UNDERSTAND THE FUNDAMENTALS OF INVESTING AND WATCH YOUR MONEY GROW

Some personal finance books dive right into investing. In fact, you can get books that focus only on investing. Some financial advisors and authors make investing seem glamorous and even easy. Use money to make money. Invest it, then sit back and become rich. Truthfully, most financial matters aren't that simple.

I've already told you that I'm a big proponent of taking things slowly and building up savings before investing. I put this chapter at the end, not because I don't see it as important, but because I advise having some other finance fundamentals in place first. The danger of losing money is too great and I fall on the side of protecting your money.

Before you have money to invest, you must *earn*. Then you must *save*. Once you have savings, then you can *invest*. Investing is using money to make money. It's reallocating money into places where it will grow into more.

We've been focusing on personal finance rules that are more important for you than investing, I believe. Before a young Steph Curry learned trick shots, he learned that he couldn't run with the ball without dribbling. Lionel Messi learned that he couldn't touch the soccer ball with his hands before he perfected penalty kicks. Jeff Gordon stood in line at the DMV as a teenager to get his learner's permit, before he became a racing champion.

Now ask yourself: Am I ready to take the next step? Review this list of questions:

Are my credit cards and high-interest loans paid off?

Do I have proper insurance for myself, home, and cars?

Do I have emergency savings?

Am I saving for retirement?

Is my remaining debt (home, car, student loans) under control?

Am I ready to watch my money grow?

If you answered no to any of these questions, then go fix that first. If you can answer yes to all, then you're ready to explore investing.

I've chosen to point you to fundamentals that you will use for a lifetime: accumulate money to meet your needs; stay out of bad debt; and build your emergency fund. Once you've met those basic needs—congratulations! *Now* it's time to talk about investing and doing it the right way so that you hold onto the precious money you've worked so hard to accumulate. It doesn't matter what investment rate you get if you don't have money to invest. Let's first define typical investments and look at the typical investment time horizon for each.

Types of Investments

Type	Definition	Time Horizon
Alternative investments	Describes investments that are outside of standard asset classes (commodities, currencies, derivatives, oil & gas, etc.)	Long-term
Annuities	Financial contract that provides specific payments at a future date	Long-term
Balanced mutual funds	Pooled investment fund that diversifies equally in stocks and bonds	Mid-term
Bonds	Loans made to companies in exchange for interest and return of principal	Long-term
Bond index funds	Mutual fund that mirrors bond market holdings	Mid-term
Small business investments	Independently owned and operated company	Long-term
Cash	Legal tender or coins used to purchase goods or services	Short-term
Certificates of deposit	Promissory note issued by a bank for a specific term	Short- or mid-term
Exchange-traded funds	Similar to a mutual fund that mirrors an index, but trades like a stock	Long-term
Life insurance	Financial contract that pays heirs when an insured dies; can provide for tax-deferred investment growth	Long-term

Money market accounts	Type of savings account that offers market interest rates of return	Short-term
Municipal bonds	Local government bonds issued by states, municipalities, and counties	Long-term
Mutual funds	Pooled investment fund that diversifies in various stocks and/or bonds	Long-term
Real estate	Real property held to produce income and/or to appreciate in value	Long-term
Savings accounts	Bank account that pays interest on the amount invested	Short- or mid-term
Savings bonds	Small denomination government bonds issued by the US Treasury	Short-term
Stock index funds	Mutual fund that mirrors stock market holdings	Mid-term
Stocks	Equity ownership of a company in the form of a share	Long-term
Treasury bonds	Government bonds issued by the US Treasury	Mid- or long-term

Let me explain some safe places to invest and some fundamental principles that have a low risk of failure and high risk of making a profit. You can't go wrong with retirement accounts, a modest home or condo, and safe investment choices.

RETIREMENT ACCOUNTS

Retirement accounts are great for accumulating wealth to be used later in life. I would strongly advise you to take full advantage of accounts offered through your employer or open an Individual Retirement Account (IRA) of your own. You can decide how risky you want to be with investments, and if you start investing when you are young, you will have decades to watch your money grow.

Employer plans, such as 401(k) plans, have unique advantages that can super-charge your ability to accumulate wealth during your career. The maximum amount that you can contribute in 2018, according to the government, is $18,500 a year. If you can afford that, take full advantage of setting aside that amount for retirement. If that's too much or if you're just starting out with saving toward retirement, I encourage you to build up to at least 10 percent of your salary. Some investment firms have programs that allow you to automatically increase your investments by 1 percent of your salary each year.

Many employers provide further incentives by matching a portion of your contribution. If you can invest in an employer plan, don't miss out on this free money that your employer is willing to give you each and every year. For example, if you choose to invest 3 percent of your salary, your company might also contribute 3 percent. Now, 6 percent of your annual salary is being invested toward your retirement. Combining your contribution with an employer match will make that fund grow quickly.

In addition to getting free money from your employer, these plans offer tax breaks. As explained in the previous chapter, the money you put into these retirement accounts does not get taxed until you retire and start using the money. You lower your tax bill for every dollar you put into your retirement plan. Plus, all the earnings and increases of the money in your plan are also tax-deferred. That means you don't pay tax on the gains until you start using it in retirement. Many plans also offer loan options, allowing you to borrow from yourself in the case of a sudden hardship.

Let me point out some specific options you have for retirement investments:

401(k) – This is a retirement account offered through some employers. Opening a 401(k) is a reliable and safe way to invest toward retirement.

403(b) – This is similar to a 401(k) but offered through non-profit, religious, and government organizations.

Traditional IRA – If you are self-employed or your employer does not offer a retirement benefit, you can open your own IRA through an investment firm. You are allowed the same deduction benefits and tax deferral. Limits are lower, at $5,500 per year. The money still grows over time tax-free.

Roth IRA – This is a specific type of IRA. You don't get current tax deductions, but all the money you invest, plus the earnings, are tax-free when you use it in retirement. It's a question of paying taxes now or later. These come with income limits, so they aren't available to everyone, but they might be worth considering. You can open a Roth IRA in addition to a 401(k).

SEP IRA or Solo 401(k) – Simplified Employee Pension (SEP) or solo accounts are an option for self-employed individuals or business owners. These plans offer many of the same tax deductions and tax-deferral opportunities.

If you are not sure which retirement investment account is right for you, consult your company's Human Resources department or ask a trusted financial advisor.

One note about waiting for investing: If you work for an employer that will match retirement funds, take advantage of that free money even if you don't have your budget prepared or your savings in place. Contribute as much as you need to from your salary to receive all the free matching money that your employer will fund. Then continue to put the other financial principles into place before investing more.

REAL ESTATE

Everybody wants a great house. Home ownership is part of the American dream. Buying a home can be a great financial decision if you buy one that you can afford in an area where real estate is increasing in value. Historically, home prices have tended to appreciate, so chances are good that you can make a profit when you sell the house. Real estate has yielded positive returns for most purchasers.

Though the United States has certainly faced economic and housing crises that have negatively affected homeowners, owning a home is still a good investment for most people. It might be a good time to consider real estate as an investment.

I'll offer a few guidelines that usually indicate that buying a house is a good choice:

- You're in a location where you want to live for a while.

- You're in a location with many job opportunities. This indicates that the community is growing, and people will be interested in buying homes when you're ready to sell.

- Your monthly mortgage payment will be close to or less than what you're paying in rent.

- You have solid credit and can find a competitive interest rate from a lender.

- You're ready for the stress of home ownership and maintenance.

- Your family is growing and you need more space.

For many Americans, a large portion of their net worth is in their home. It's usually the most expensive thing you'll ever own. You certainly need to do your research and talk with a trusted real estate agent, but for most people owning a home is a good investment.

I counsel professional athlete clients not to jump into large real estate transactions. Professional sports teams control the athletes' contracts and can trade or waive a player at almost any time. That makes it riskier to purchase a home. I tell pros that if they really must purchase something, then get a condo or modest home they could easily sell when the time comes to move.

Depending on how your experience goes with home ownership, you might also consider purchasing real estate as an investment to produce income. If the area is right, a rental property can bring in extra income for you and your family. I like real estate as an income-producing investment because it's something I can relate to and understand. You and I have lived this business—literally. If you own a home, then you understand the business and maintenance involved in owning another home that you'll rent to others.

Real estate is a popular investment choice for professional athletes. I've talked with many who buy not only homes for themselves, but also rental properties, land, or sometimes whole apartment complexes. Owning property can be profitable, but I've seen people lose money in real estate, too. As with any financial decision, you must move slowly and cautiously and do your research. Realtors emphasize "location, location, location," and I would add "timing." If you're ready, this could be a great investment for you.

SAFE INVESTMENTS

You often hear professional athletes talk about how they have to adapt their game plan depending on their opponent. They change their strategy, utilize different teammates, and adjust their plays to increase the likelihood that they win. We also must understand what we are trying to accomplish and implement the best investment strategy we can to succeed.

The best strategies to use are good financial habits. Implement these plays and you will understand the basics of investing:

Habitual contributions

Dollar-cost averaging

Diversification

Time horizons

Habitual contributions – Wherever you're investing, do it regularly. Make it an automatic contribution. A good example of this is your 401(k). Through your employer, you can have a certain amount of money automatically added each pay period. The money is bypassing your bank account and being saved and invested. Such programmed saving can really add up. You can do this with almost any bank account—automatically send a certain amount of money to your investment account.

Dollar-cost averaging – As a result of programming your savings, you can buy investments regularly and get the benefits of dollar-cost averaging. This means that you're purchasing shares of investments, usually mutual funds, periodically, and getting the benefit of market fluctuations. You are investing a specific dollar amount each time. When the market is low, that fixed amount is buying more shares. When the market is high, you're buying fewer shares. This method takes some worry out of investing and being at the mercy of the ups and downs of investment markets.

Diversification – Diversification is the strategy of making different kinds of investments so that you are not over-exposed to risks. The economy, markets, and investments tend to go in cycles and fluctuate over time. If you heavily invest in one area and that sector has a downturn, your loss could be great. However, if you spread your risks out over many different sectors, you don't get hit as hard by a downturn in any area. You don't want all your money in one investment.

Time horizons – This refers to investing appropriately for when you'll need the money. If you're young and investing for retirement way into the future, you can be more aggressive in stock-based investments, which have a little more risk and usually generate more favorable returns over a long period of time. As you come closer to retirement, be more conservative so you don't risk losing that money.

If you have a short-term horizon for when you need the money, then you need to be invested in something that is liquid, meaning that you can convert it to cash quickly and inexpensively. For example, a tech stock could be a great long-term investment, but during that time horizon the stock could have volatile periods where it goes up 40 percent and where it goes down that much. If you will need your money in a year, you wouldn't want to put it in that tech stock. The risk is too great that it would be down, and you wouldn't have the money you need. The chart below depicts some time horizons and the types of investment that would generally be most appropriate.

Category	Time Span	Typical Investments
Short-term	0-3 years	Cash Savings accounts Money market accounts Certificates of deposit Savings bonds
Medium-term	3-10 years	Savings accounts Certificates of deposit Balanced mutual funds Bond index funds Stock index funds Treasury bonds
Long-term	10 or more years	Stocks Bonds Mutual funds Exchange-traded funds Municipal bonds Treasury bonds Real estate Annuities Life insurance Small businesses Alternative investments

Your investments should reflect how soon you need the money.

DON'T TRY TO DO TOO MUCH

If you've been wise with your money and you're thinking of investing, you've done the right thing! You've gotten to the point where you have money to invest, and that's great. You've been hitting singles, so keep hitting singles. Don't go for home runs that might lead to strikeouts.

What I mean by this is that you've made small, steady, and smart steps to keep yourself financially strong. That's a great pattern to continue. Don't get reckless or hurried into an investment that might be costly. You can win ballgames hitting consistent singles!

The world of investing can be intimidating. There are articles and television shows telling you constantly that you can do it yourself. Unfortunately, you can easily lead yourself down the wrong path. It is OK to seek professional help with investing.

Also, use common sense and invest in moderation. Move cautiously into investments, especially if:

It seems too good to be true.

It could hurt your monthly budget.

It requires a lot of cash flow.

Your investment will be locked up for an unknown amount of time.

You're not working with qualified professionals.

Learn all you can, pace yourself, and seek out the experts who can help guide you, and you'll win at investing, too.

Turning to my history with basketball, it wouldn't matter if I had a great three-point shot if half the time I dribbled the ball up the court, it bounced off my foot and went out of bounds. If I can't even get the shot off, then my ability to shoot is useless! Investments don't mean anything if you don't get to the point of investing. Smart practices like budgeting and saving get you to the point of investing.

Anyone can score a financial touchdown if they make a few good choices. That doesn't mean that everyone will be rich by society's terms, but it does mean that you can be comfortable and protected through most phases of life. Follow these rules and you'll be an all-star in my book. Make money, save money, spend and invest wisely. Touchdown!

—— PLAYBOOK ——

RULE 7: STICK TO SAFE INVESTMENTS

KEY FUNDAMENTALS:
Take advantage of retirement accounts
Consider smart real estate investments
Invest safely and securely

TAKE IT FROM A PRO

My thought process was always very conservative. I think my Dad instilled in me to appreciate the things I had and work hard for my money. He taught me not to spend foolishly on material things. That has stuck with me pretty well. Once I started making money, I started saving and got a financial advisor.

With investments, my approach has always been growth and being conservative so that in 20, 30, 40 years that money has grown.

- Garrett Jones, Major League Baseball (MLB) (1999-2016)

Conclusion: Game Time

Now that you know some fundamental rules of the finance game, it's time for you to play, and, of course, to win! Think about the game of professional football. Coaches continually teach a variety of plays with different iterations throughout the summer. They are planning for the fall season when they hope their team performs well and comes away with victories. The coaches design, practice, and eventually call the plays they think will be the most successful.

After the coaches do their jobs, it's up to the athletes to execute the plays. If everyone on the team does his job, the team will gain yardage on the field. A successful play does not always end up scoring a touchdown. Some plays are designed to get only one yard. On a fourth-and-goal situation, anything but a touchdown would be a failure. The key is that the team runs the play to the best of its ability when it counts.

You have a playbook that has winning financial plays in it. You've read my advice and the stories, insight, and advice from sports legends. It's time for you to start practicing these fundamentals and begin making better personal financial decisions. You will have both small and possibly big financial decisions to make in the very near future, so you will have the opportunity to try out these proven plays on your own personal finances. It's your turn to get in the game.

It may take some time to get good at running the plays in this book. You may need to go back and re-read certain sections. You may have to practice tracking your expenses, refining your budget, and analyzing your net worth calculations. You might want to make adjustments. But that's what makes victory so much sweeter. You can succeed and improve your financial situation. Winning is within your grasp. Quitting should not be an option.

As you start to make progress and improve your decision-making, be sure to acknowledge your wins. I don't mean that you should reward frugal spending by splurging. What I mean is to celebrate your accomplishment in a way that provides you with positive reinforcement. Keeping score by charting the gains in your net worth may inspire you to accumulate even more financial victories. Seeing your bank account value increase, watching your credit card debt go down, and lowering your monthly outlays all are victories. Look up at the scoreboard and recognize your success. Get on a winning streak for yourself and your future.

Touchdown Finance is about guiding you to financial success and peace of mind. I wrote this book so you can learn from the rules outlined in each chapter, combined with the tales of the "thrill of victory" and the "agony of defeat." I want you to know where your money is going, to be wise financially, and to avoid the pitfalls that others have made.

The ball is in your hands now. The brisk fall air fills your lungs. You see the obstacles but also the goal line. It's time for YOU to run for the end zone to score a touchdown in your personal finances. Good luck!

Acknowledgements

Thank you to Leslie Caldwell who learned a new language of personal finance to bring this book to fruition. Her talent was on display as she took the stories of pros and made them so much more interesting than the author could have done! She made this book happen with her persistence and drive.

Thank you to my wife, Teresa, and children, Kevin, Nathan, Lauren, and Jacob. Their support, encouragement, and love are boundless and have pushed me to use my experience and expertise to coach others in making better financial decisions. Kevin, an admitted non-reader, said that he *could not put down* an early draft of the book and read it in one sitting. This helped affirm that the mix of personal finance and sports could be entertaining and educational, and that this book could reach those who love sports but who may not know much about personal finance.

Thank you to Dan Fitzpatrick, a long-time friend and former options trader, who helped provide a professional's viewpoint along with his common-sense perspectives and vast experiences in personal finance.

Thank you, the reader, for taking steps to improve your personal finance acumen and for investing your time to read this book.

Of course, thank you to the current and former professional athletes I have had the pleasure of getting to know. Gaining knowledge from the legends of the game has been such a blessing. Even though many lessons from pro athletes have been what *not* to do, their willingness to share their stories with the world has accelerated my learning and helped shape the advice I share today. Tips from the pros are truly nuggets of wisdom that I cherish.

I want to give special thanks to the following pros and friends who took time out of their busy schedules to offer words of wisdom to the readers of this book:

Jerry Harkness was my Amateur Athletic Union (AAU) coach in the mid-1980s in Indianapolis. Before I knew him, he was a basketball star at Loyola University Chicago. He won the NCAA championship in 1963 and later played professionally in the NBA for the New York Knicks and the Indiana Pacers. Having devoted much of his life to civil rights issues, he has a lot to teach us, on and off the court.

Kirani James, sprinter, is an Olympic gold and silver track medalist and world champion in the 400 meters. A graduate and track star from the University of Alabama, Kirani was the first Grenadian to win an Olympic medal.

Lindsay Whalen began her WNBA career with the Connecticut Sun before moving to the Minnesota Lynx, with whom she has four WNBA championships. She has also won World Championships and Olympic gold with the US women's basketball team.

Graham Gano is an All-Pro placekicker in the NFL. He has played for the Baltimore Ravens, Washington Redskins, and Carolina Panthers. Graham has built a strong career through hard work and dedication to the sport.

Ian Mahinmi is an NBA champion who has played for the San Antonio Spurs, Dallas Mavericks, Indiana Pacers, and Washington Wizards. From France, he also has a notable basketball career overseas.

Brian Carroll is a retired defensive midfielder who built a 14-year career with Major League Soccer. He played for DC United and Columbus Crew before moving to the Philadelphia Union where he finished his pro soccer career. He is now a respected financial planner.

Garrett Jones has been a professional baseball player for 18 years. In Major League Baseball, he played for the Minnesota Twins, Pittsburgh Pirates, Miami Marlins, and New York Yankees. He continued his professional career in Japan as a first baseman and right fielder.

About the Author

Dr. John Karaffa understands sports and taxes, which is the perfect combination for this book. He's a Butler Bulldog at heart. That's where he played college basketball before competing for twelve seasons professionally overseas. While playing in Germany, he used his accounting degree at a Big 4 global tax firm and now has more than thirty years of experience in the industry.

After his professional basketball career, John realized the need for tax accountants who understand the unique challenges faced by professional athletes. He founded and is the President of ProSport CPA, a Virginia-based accounting firm. ProSport CPA is the leading tax firm in professional sports, serving more than 500 clients from all major leagues.

John is a sought-after speaker about sports tax and has been featured in publications such as *GQ, Accounting Today, Journal of Accountancy, Bloomberg Tax, Nerd Wallet, Fox Business,* and *Global Sports Law and Taxation Reports.*

If John is not at the office or at home with his wife and four kids, you might find him on a basketball court in his community or joining a group of friends for pick-up games. He'll never lose his love for sports.